Someone I Love Has Died:

Grief is a Journey of Discovery

by Andrew Lindwall

Illustrations by
Emily Weyel

Foreword by
Ted Lindwall

Someone I Love Has Died: Grief is a Journey of Discovery© 2017 by Andrew Lindwall

All Rights Reserved. No part of this publication may be reproduced, stored in a retrieval system, or transmitted in any form or by any means, electronic, mechanical, recording, or otherwise, without the prior written permission of the individual author or the publisher.

Published by RHEMA Publishing House.™
rhemapublishinghouse.com
PO Box 1244 McKinney, TX 75070

For information about special discounts available for bulk purchases, sales promotions, and educational needs, contact RHEMA Publishing House at the above address.

This book is not intended as a substitute for the medical advice of physicians. The reader should consult a physician in matters related to his/her health and particularly with respect to any symptoms that may require diagnosis or medical attention. The author assumes no responsibility for any reader's attempts to self-diagnose any medical condition.

Scripture quotations are from the ESV® Bible (The Holy Bible, English Standard Version®), copyright © 2001 by Crossway, a publishing ministry of Good News Publishers. Used by permission. All rights reserved.

ISBN: 978-0-9983064-9-0
ebook ISBN: 978-0-9990932-0-7

Cover Design: Janie Owen-Bugh

Dedicated to Lito –
My grandfather, mentor, role model, friend.

Written for grieving children, ages 3-99,
and for those who walk this journey
with them.

Table of Contents
Foreword by Lito

Introducing the "Helping Grieving Children" Series 1

Other titles in the series 3

Someone I Love Has Died:
 Grief is a Journey of Discovery 6

You Are Not Alone 10

Sometimes You Will Feel Lonely 13

Everybody Takes a Different Path 16

You Can't Always See Around Every Bend 20

You Must Keep Going; and You Can! 23

There are Lots of Things to Discover Along the Way ... 27

Your Final Destination May Look Different Than
 What You First Imagined 33

About the Author 39

About the Illustrator 40

About Journey of Hope Grief Support Centers 41

Endnotes 42

Foreword
by Andrew's Real Live Grandfather

When Andrew was only four years old, his father, my son Timothy, died after several years of illness. This was a hard and confusing time for Andrew and caused him to think much about what was happening.

Now, years later, Andrew writes a story about things he learned—from me, from other members of the family, from his own careful thinking, and, I believe, from God as well. He and I hope his story will be a help to you as well.

Lito

(Pronounced "LEE toe"—a shortened Spanish nickname from Abuelo or Abuelito which means "Granddad").

Introducing the
"Helping Grieving Children"
Series
by **RHEMA Publishing House**

Walking alongside children and their caregivers who have experienced the devastating loss of a loved one is a special privilege! Knowing that we can help them to grieve well and work through and reconcile that loss in a way that brings healing and strength—as part of their new self and "new normal"—just makes life worth living!

- 1 in 5 children experience the death of someone close to them by age 18.[1]
- Studies from various countries on childhood bereavement following parental death report that children in this situation do experience a wide range of emotional and behavioral symptoms… The child often experiences an increase in anxiety with a focus on concerns about further loss, the safety of other family members, and fears around separation.[2]
- 7 in 10 classroom teachers (69%) currently have at least one student in their class(es) who has lost a parent, guardian, or close friend in the past year. They report that students who have lost a parent or guardian typically exhibit:

- Difficulty concentrating in class
- Withdrawal/disengagement and less class participation
- Absenteeism
- Decrease in quality of work
- Less reliability in turning in assignments[3]

The featured mini-booklets in the "Helping Grieving Children Series" were written for children everywhere who struggle to work through the myriad emotions felt and behaviors exhibited after losing a loved one.

Other Titles in the Series:

1. **Someone I Love Has Died: Everyone Grieves AND No One Grieves Like Me!** was written to describe grief as universal, and yet, so very unique to each person. Everybody grieves after the death of someone close, but one individual's pain and sorrow isn't ever "better" or "worse" than another's.

2. **Someone I Love Has Died: Get Me OFF This Emotional Roller-Coaster Called GRIEF!** describes life as FILLED with crazy twists and turns, scary ups and downs, unpredictable, and sometimes very hard times—like a roller-coaster—especially after someone you love has died. You will be okay, you will survive, and you may just come out a hero!

3. **Someone I Love Has Died: Now What do I DO?** encourages helpers and children to attend to the seven tasks of embracing emotions and reconciling mourning.

4. **Someone I Love Has Died: Grief is a Journey of Discovery.** The steps of grief and mourning are like going on a difficult journey, and the path you take and your final destination may look quite different than what you imagined. Through it all, you can keep going—and you will!

5. **Someone I Love Has Died: Traditions & Rituals & Services, OH MY!** Everyone is gathering around and talking about going to funerals and memorial services and activities! Let's talk about what's going on before, during, and after these services and the part you can take throughout the visits and services.

6. **Someone I Love Has Died: Was it My Fault?** Many times, after someone you love gets hurt or dies, you will often have thoughts that it might have been your fault: "If only I had___!" But it is NOT your fault that someone you love has died. Let me tell you how I know this is true!

7. **Someone I Love Has Died: Why Can't I Meet My New Brother or Sister?** explains miscarriage and stillbirth and how to help children understand what happens when a baby is lost in the womb and how to grieve that loss.

You can find more titles in the Helping Grieving Children Series at
http://rhemapublishinghouse.com/helping-grieving-children/

Someone I Love Has Died:
Grief is a Journey of Discovery
✼✼✼

Andrew felt all alone in the world. His daddy had died, and this was the first time Andrew had ever experienced a death. He was confused by his situation and scared by this new concept. It was so very strange to think he would never see his daddy again, never talk to him, never play with him, never pray with him... And it brought up so many other thoughts too: if daddy could die, couldn't anybody else? Andrew's mother said the funeral was lovely, but it just made him sadder.

Why did everyone want to keep talking and thinking about daddy when it just broke your heart more? Uncles and aunts, grandparents, family friends, daddy's coworkers and other people all stood up and talked about how great daddy was, and everyone cried when they talked about him. It was all just so confusing why everyone put themselves through that pain, and it made Andrew sad and angry. So, when Lito asked what was wrong and Andrew told him, Lito suggested they go for a walk in the woods to clear their heads.

"Andrew," Lito said, "It is okay to feel sad at a funeral. It's quite natural; in fact, that is pretty much the reason we have a funeral."

"To feel sad?" Andrew asked, a bit flustered. His grandfather opened the back door for him, and they both crossed the back yard and started walking along the path through the woods that led back to the river.

"Well, the funeral is not designed to make you sad." Lito explained. "It is planned to celebrate the life of the loved-one who has died. And everyone will react to that celebration in a different way, and there is nothing wrong with that. Some will cry, some will be angry, some will just stare and listen and won't seem to react at all. Everyone has a different way of handling the funeral, just as they have a different way of handling the journey from here on out."

Andrew jumped over a fallen tree, and while he waited for Lito to step gingerly over, he asked, "What journey? Are we all going somewhere after the funeral?"

"Life is the journey, Andrew," Lito said when he was over the tree. "We've all been traveling it together, and now we have to figure out how that journey is going to look without your father coming along with us. The journey is a lot like this wooded path we're walking. When I was a young boy, I walked this path with my father. When your father was a young boy, he walked this path with me, just like you walked with your father, and someday you may well walk this path with your son."

Andrew picked up a stick along the path and swung it at the tall weeds. "Now that daddy is gone, are you going to walk the path with me?"

When you go through

DEEP WATERS

I will be with you...
Isaiah 43:2 NLT

You Are Not Alone

"I will walk this path with you," Lito smiled. "As long as we can! That is one of the lovely things about this journey we must walk— we don't have to walk it alone.

"The journey is a difficult or hard one, because you are so used to walking it with your father, and now you must discover or find out for yourself what it means to walk the same path without him. And that can be a very discouraging thing, but remember—just because your father isn't here to walk with you doesn't mean nobody is here to walk with you.

"Just like everyone has their own reaction to the funeral, everyone also has their own way of walking this journey. Some of us prefer to walk alone, and that's okay. Some of us need to have someone walk with us, and that's okay. And some of us will need a whole group to walk with us, and that's okay, too."

Lito put his hand on Andrew's shoulder and leaned on him as they walked up a steep hill.

"Don't be afraid to ask your loved ones for help along the way if you need it. If I didn't have your help to get up this hill, my journey would end at the bottom there—or I would take a really long time and it would be a lot more work to get over the hill. I need help to get to the top, and that is the beauty of walking this path with someone.

"If you need help, that someone is there to help you along, and you are there to help that someone along, too.

"The journey is like that. There are times along the way that are very difficult for you; sometimes you may not be able to get through without help. That is what family is for—we help each other out in our times of need. We make the journey easier for each other."

Sometimes You Will Feel Lonely

because you're not used to taking this path without your loved one.

Andrew and Lito stopped at the top of the hill and took in the view for a moment.

"I miss him," Andrew almost whispered. "We would always stop here and try to see the river through those trees. Sometimes we would see deer on the other side, but they were always gone by the time we got to the river."

"I miss him, too," Lito gave Andrew a hug. "You and your father had your routine, things you did every time you walked this path. Now on your journey as you walk on without him, you will continue to do a lot of the things you used to do together. And when you do them without him, you will remember what it was like when he was here.

"It can be a very sad time, a very lonely time, learning to travel your journey without someone you love. We grow so used to our journey with our loved ones, that when they can no longer journey with us, it is very hard to handle. It can be very lonely for you, or sometimes it can be very soothing."

"How can it be lonely AND soothing?"

"Well, as for me, I used to walk this path with your father when he was your age. Now I'm walking this path with you, and I remember the times I walked with him. So, I am making new memories with you, but I am also reliving good memories I have of him. It makes me sad that I'll never walk with my son again, but I am grateful for the times I did get to walk with him. The good memories make it less lonely for me... Help me walk down this hill."

Everybody Takes a Different Path
❧❧❧

At the bottom of the hill, the path ran along a dry creek-bed. Andrew used his stick as a walking stick and held onto tree branches so he could climb down into the creek-bed.

"Come on, Lito!" Andrew called, "Let's walk down here for a bit!"

"You go ahead," Lito replied. "I'll walk along behind you, here on the path. I'll be here if you need me. Even with your help, I don't think I could get down there, or back out.

"On the journey, everyone walks a different path too—based on what we can and can't handle, those we have who can help us along, and generally by finding what path works best for us.

"We're all made differently, and we can't all take the same path. Sometimes, it is just too difficult for me to take the same path as you, and sometimes, you would get more out of the experience of a different path—like your creek-bed—than I would.

"On your journey, you will find that some things are better for you to do, and other people taking the same journey have other ideas. There is nothing wrong with that, of course. We all must find the things in life that help us cope with our situations.

"You may find when you're sad and thinking about your father, it helps you unwind to play baseball. Your mother probably wouldn't enjoy baseball too much but would find help and hope in reading the Bible or another book. And I would prefer to sit by the pond and watch the fish or water my garden.

"See, all of us would do different things to help ourselves through the emotional struggle of all of these sad feelings, but we would all do things that would help us as individuals in ways that are best for us. Of course, there are some things we would all enjoy, like playing a card game together, sharing a meal, watching a movie, or like right now, taking a walk together.

"So, you see, we all must take a different path, even though we're all trying to get to the same place—and luckily there are many places along the way where our paths intersect. We just have to work together and communicate or talk about ways to find where those helpful places are."

"I think I understand," Andrew said, walking under a bridge as Lito was walking along the top. Climbing out of the creek-bed and back up to the path, Andrew took Lito's hand and asked, "So you said we're all trying to get to the same place. Where is that?"

The LORD is nigh unto them that are of a Broken heart; and saveth such as be of a contrite spirit.
Psalm 34:18 KJV

You Can't Always See Around Every Bend

Lito stopped walking, and looked all around in a circle. "Which way is the house from here?" he asked. Andrew looked around in a circle and realized he wasn't entirely sure.

"I think it's that way," Andrew pointed. "I'm not sure, but the path is a pretty big circle. After the river, we walk through the woods on the other side, and then behind the neighbor's field and back to the house."

Lito smiled. "So we'll keep walking along the path, and we're sure to get back to the house. I suppose it doesn't matter what direction it is in. We can't see where the house is, but we know if we follow this path, we'll get to where we're trying to go.

"It is the same with the journey. The road winds, turns, circles, backtracks, goes over creeks, and under bridges, through the trees, and over hills. We can't always see around the bend. We don't always know what we are going to come across in the road, but we are sure the road is going to lead us where we're trying to go.

"Or," Lito chuckled, "Rather, the road is going to lead us where the good Lord wants us to go. Sometimes the destination God has in store for us is not quite the one we had planned for ourselves. It is faith that keeps us walking on the journey. *Faith tells us we will get to the destination, even though we can't always see it when we're walking this winding road.*"

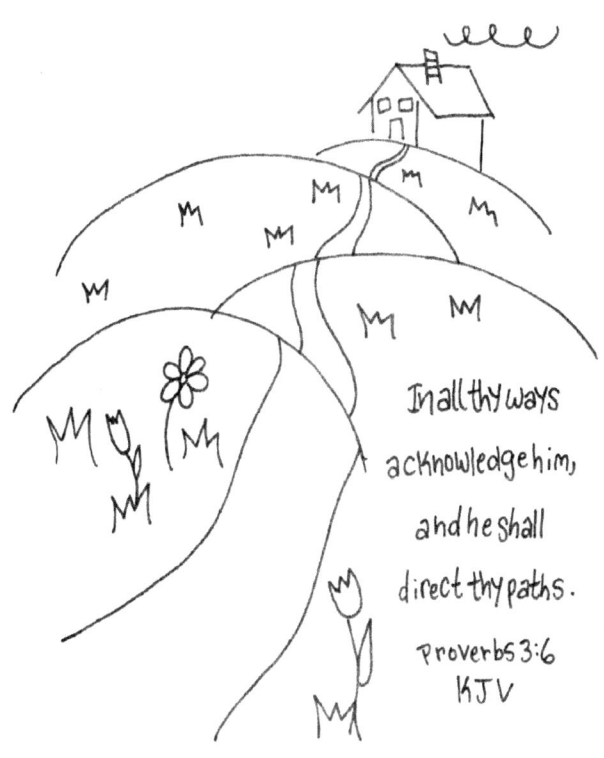

You Must Keep Going; And You Can!

At the end of a sharp turn on the path they were walking, there was a large pile of trees in the road that had been bunched up there in the last rainstorm. The whole road was blocked, and the woods were thick on either side.

"Come on," Lito beckoned, "We'll go through the woods a little way, just to get around this obstacle."

"But the trees are really thick," Andrew protested, "And there are stickers, and thorns, and chiggers..."

"Well, you are right, but we have to keep going." Lito lifted a tree branch over his head and disappeared into the woods. Andrew quickly followed so he wouldn't be left alone. As Lito walked through the branches and tall grass, he explained. "There will be obstacles like that buildup of brush on your journey. There are obstacles like that on everyone's journey. But you must keep going. You must progress, or you will never make it to your destination.

"Many people decide at those points that the way is too hard, and all the alternatives—other choices—are too hard as well. Those are the people who sit, and wallow, and stagnate. They don't finish their journey, and they will never find a way to live without the loved-ones they've lost. That is not healthy. You **must–keep–going**; **and you can**!

"All the ways we had to walk were going to be difficult, and very likely were going to be uncomfortable as well. We could have climbed over that pile of trees, or we could do as we are and walk through the thick woods, or we could backtrack until we found an alternate route. But we mustn't give up just because we think the journey is too hard.

"The journey is hard for a reason—so, we will be stronger when we have finished. Do not pity or feel sorry for yourself for the difficult journey you must travel, but look at what you learn from the struggle, and notice how much easier the same obstacle is the second time you come across it."

The view is beautiful at the top.

There Are Lots of Things to Discover Along the Way
about yourself and about the
person who died

Lito moved one more branch, and held it up so Andrew could walk through. They found themselves on the other side of the brush pile, back on the pathway.

"The obstacles get easier each time?" Andrew asked as they began walking again.

"They can, and they often do." Lito patted Andrew on the shoulder. "How you handle the obstacles, and learn from them each time, will teach you a lot about yourself."

Andrew looked confused. "I already know myself. I AM myself!"

"So you do, and so you are." Lito answered. "But you are young, you still have growing to do; and as much as you think you won't change, you very well might! I'm 62 years old, and I still change, and I still grow!

"I learned a lot about myself when my father died, and I think I will learn a lot about myself again now that my son has died.

"Along this journey you will learn all sorts of things about yourself. You'll learn that certain things bug or annoy you that never did before. You'll learn how patient you can be with people who do not understand what you are going through. You will learn how compassionate you can be with people who go through your same situations, now that you know how bad it felt for you when you went through them.

"You'll learn how strong you are, how weak you are, how emotional you are, how nice, how thoughtful, how scatterbrained, how, how, how... Everything is likely to change, for this is a life-altering event. These are the events in life that change us, that shape us to be the people the Lord has planned for us to become. How you handle the situation and how you let it mold you—how you grow—determines the kind of person you are when you reach your destination." Lito stopped walking and looked to the left side of the path.

"Look over there." He pointed off the path, down a very steep hill to a sheer cliff that dropped into the pond. "Suppose you and your friends were out here on the path, and they decided it would be fun to run down this hill and jump off the ledge into the water."

"That's a pretty long drop..." Looking uncomfortable, Andrew peered down into the water from their path, far above.

"It is, and let's just imagine you were afraid of heights. You probably wouldn't want to go jumping off any cliffs, even though you see your friends doing it and seem to be having fun and no one is getting hurt; they're just jumping into the water and swimming!

"In that situation, you might learn something about yourself. You might learn that, while you like hanging out with your friends, you are not easily swayed when you've decided you don't want to do something.

"You might learn that you would like to join them, but when you get to the cliff, you just can't bring yourself to jump off, even though you'd like to. You might learn that even though you are afraid of heights, you enjoy the thrill of that fear and force yourself to jump off anyway and find that you have fun in the process. Or you might learn that after your first jump, you aren't afraid of heights after all.

"My point is, you'll be put in a lot of situations now that a loved-one has died. People do not often know how to react to someone who is in your situation, and they very often say and do things that will upset you, despite their best intentions. It is in these happenstances, when these things happen, that you will learn things about yourself, because it is in these times that you will be reacting to new experiences for the first time, and you may surprise yourself with how you react.

"These are learning experiences. Use them to learn about yourself and to grow. Use them so that when you experience these situations again, you will have an idea of what you think is the appropriate and best way to respond, and you will be able to grow and to teach yourself how to respond best."

"Well, when you put it that way, I guess I could learn some things about myself." Andrew started walking down the path again, and Lito followed.

Your Final Destination May Look Different Than What You First Imagined

When they reached the river, Andrew looked expectantly over the edge and gave an exasperated sigh.

Lito asked him, "What's the matter?"

"There's not as much water as I thought there would be," Andrew grumbled. "I like to watch the water flow, but the river is so low there are just a few puddles; none of the water is running."

Lito looked down into the river and saw that Andrew was right. There was no running water—just a beaver dam in the middle of some standing water, a turtle on top of a log, and small frogs in the mud.

"That is unfortunate," Lito agreed. "That is the way of things—sometimes your destination just looks different than what you first imagined. Your journey is like that too."

Andrew turned from the river and started walking back to the path. "How is that?"

Lito followed, and the two began their trek from the river back to the house.

"We all might have an idea of what life will look like without our loved-one. You think since your dad isn't around anymore, your mother may have to work more and you won't see her as much; or sometime down the road she may remarry and your family dynamic will change; or your family may have to move somewhere else; or your family traditions and daily routine may become quite different.

"You look at all these differences that may be occurring in your life and you follow them through to how you think they will affect the rest of your life. That can be quite an upsetting line of thought.

"Now, while the future is an important topic—and it is something you need to think about and prepare for—just know that no one can see or know the future, and the good Lord has a plan for you. There is a difference between preparing or planning for the future, and worrying about the future.

"You may look at your grieving process for your father and wonder how it will look ten years from now. Will you still cry when you visit his grave? Will you still think about how iced tea was his favorite drink, just as it is yours? Will you still sing the same song the two of you did when you played baseball? Will you even still play baseball anymore, now that he's not here to play it with you?

"You can have ideas about what all of this is going to look like in the future, but you need to understand that grief is not a predictable thing. You may set a timetable for yourself, but don't expect that grief is going to abide by it or stick to your timetable.

"My father died almost fifty years ago now, and I still grieve, but not nearly as much. There isn't anything wrong with that. I think the best thing would be to know and understand that the end of your journey, whatever you consider that to be, probably will not look the way you expect it to, just as the river didn't look the way you expected it to. And you need to know—that's okay.

"Speaking of which, there may not be an actual *end* to the journey. And that's okay, too. My journey of grieving for my father has lasted this long, and I fully expect it to last the rest of my life—although my grief has eased over time. I fully expect to grieve for my son for the rest of my life, but I know that over time, mourning his death will be easier, will be less difficult. That works for me. You have to find what works for you—and I hope you do—and that it makes your journey that much easier to bear as well."

As Andrew and his grandfather approached the house at the end of the pathway, they stopped one last time.

"Here we are," Lito sighed. "We're at the end of the pathway. Are you ready to start your journey?"

"Yes," Andrew said, and gave him a hug.

"Thanks, I love you Lito."

"I love you, too!" Lito smiled.

About **Andrew Lindwall**

Andrew Lindwall grew up and resides in north central Texas. His most formative years were influenced greatly by men of integrity and faith—his three grandfathers, some uncles, some big brothers—and especially his father Tim, who died when Andrew was only four years old, and his second father Fred, who has loved him as his own since he was six!

Andrew has a degree in Criminology from the University of Texas, Dallas. He's served as a detention officer in Collin County, served in the Army in Germany, and is currently pursuing a degree in Cyber Security.

He's been a voracious reader and a creative writer for about fifteen years; and in this booklet he shares the story of grief and hope that is very true to his own journey.

About **Emily Weyel**

Emily Weyel is a high school student from San Antonio, Texas who now lives in Tifton, Georgia with her parents, one older sister, and five younger brothers. Emily has always enjoyed writing, painting, and doodling, so she was thrilled when she was offered the job of illustrating this series by her Aunt Karen. She has experienced grief first hand, and writing and art have always been her personal way of dealing with that grief. Emily looks forward to hopefully illustrating more books in the near future.

About **Journey of Hope Grief Support Center – Children's Grief Support Centers**

The first booklets in the "Helping Grieving Children" series were written for the Journey of Hope Grief Support Center in Plano, TX to encourage children of all ages and those who seek to serve them to grieve well and live abundant lives.

Journey of Hope was established in 1997 as a non-profit organization dedicated to providing group grief support to children, adolescents, and their parents or adult caregivers who have lost a loved-one to death. Journey of Hope offers these services in a warm, caring, and nurturing environment where the feelings of grief, pain, and loss may be expressed. Trained volunteer group facilitators lead participants in their personal journey toward healing and healthy reconciliation of their grief. You can learn more about them at http://johgriefsupport.org.

You can find children's grief support centers all over the world by searching at http://www.dougy.org/grief-support-programs/. This listing includes over 500 centers that provide grief support and services.

It is our collective desire to share these resources with grieving children in Collin and surrounding counties and all over the world!

Endnotes

[1] Kenneth Doka, Editor of OMEGA, Journal of Death and Dying. www.childrensgriefawarenessday.org

[2] Dowdney, 2000: Haine et al., 2008. www.childrensgriefawarenessday.org

[3] Grieving in Schools: Nationwide Survey among Classroom Teachers on Childhood Bereavement, conducted by New York Life Foundation and American Federation of Teachers, 2012. www.childrensgriefawarenessday.org

[4] The Lord is near to the brokenhearted and saves the crushed in spirit. Psalm 34:18 (ESV) Keep your heart with all vigilance, for from it flow the springs of life. Proverbs 4:23 (ESV)

[5] Wolfelt, 1996.

[6] from Karen's book: *Strength for the Journey*. With gratitude to Mark Hundley!

www.ingramcontent.com/pod-product-compliance
Lightning Source LLC
Chambersburg PA
CBHW070553300426
44113CB00011B/1896